From Management
to Leadership

Management Master Series

William F. Christopher
Editor in Chief

Set 4: Leadership

Burt Nanus
Leading the Way to Organization Renewal

Gabriel Hevesi
Checklist for Leaders

Karl Albrecht
Creating Leaders for Tomorrow

D. Otis Wolkins
Total Quality: A Framework for Leadership

Lawrence M. Miller
From Management to Leadership

Leonard R. Sayles
High Performance Leadership:
Creating Value in a World of Change

From Management to Leadership

Lawrence M. Miller

PRODUCTIVITY PRESS
Portland, Oregon

Management Master Series
William F. Christopher, Editor in Chief
Copyright © 1996 by Productivity Press

Productivity Press
P.O. Box 13390
Portland, OR 97213-0390
United States of America
Telephone: 503-235-0600
Telefax: 503-235-0909
E-mail: service@ppress.com

Book design by William Stanton
Cover illustration by Paul Zwolak
Page design, graphics, and composition by Rohani Design, Edmonds, Washington
Printed and bound by BookCrafters in the United States of America

Library of Congress Cataloging-in-Publication Data

Miller, Lawrence M.
    From management to leadership / Lawrence M. Miller.
        p.   cm. — (Management master series. Set 4, Leadership)
    Includes bibliographic references (pp. 70, 71).
    ISBN 1-56327-155-9. — ISBN 1-56327-103-6 (pbk.)
    1. Leadership 2. Executive ability. I. Title. II. Series.
    HD57. 7.M536   1995
    658.4' dc20   95-40110
                                                              CIP

00 99 98 97 96   10 9 8 7 6 5 4 3 2

—CONTENTS—

PUBLISHER'S MESSAGE

The *Management Master Series* was designed to discover and disseminate to you the world's best concepts, principles, and current practices in excellent management. We present this information in a concise and easy-to-use format to provide you with the tools and techniques you need to stay abreast of this rapidly accelerating world of ideas.

World class competitiveness requires managers today to be thoroughly informed about how and what other internationally successful managers are doing. What works? What doesn't? and Why?

Management is often considered a "neglected art." It is not possible to know how to manage before you are made a manager. But once you become a manager you are expected to know how to manage and to do it well, right from the start.

One result of this neglect in management training has been managers who rely on control rather than creativity. Certainly, managers in this century have shown a distinct neglect of workers as creative human beings. The idea that employees are an organization's most valuable asset is still very new. How managers can inspire and direct the creativity and intelligence of everyone involved in the work of an organization has only begun to emerge.

Perhaps if we consider management as a "science" the task of learning how to manage well will be easier. A scientist begins with an hypothesis and then runs experiments to observe whether the hypothesis is correct. Scientists depend on detailed notes about the experiment—the timing, the ingredients, the amounts—and carefully record all results as they test new hypotheses. Certain things come to be known by this method; for instance, that water always consists of one part oxygen and two parts hydrogen.

We as managers must learn from our experience and from the experience of others. The scientific approach provides a model for learning. Science begins with vision and desired outcomes, and achieves its purpose through observation, experiment, and analysis of precisely recorded results. And then what is newly discovered is shared so that each person's research will build on the work of others.

Our organizations, however, rarely provide the time for learning or experimentation. As a manager, you need information from those who have already experimented and learned and recorded their results. You need it in brief, clear, and detailed form so that you can apply it immediately.

It is our purpose to help you confront the difficult task of managing in these turbulent times. As the shape of leadership changes, the *Management Master Series* will continue to bring you the best learning available to support your own increasing artistry in the evolving science of management.

We at Productivity Press are grateful to William F. Christopher and our staff of editors who have searched out those masters with the knowledge, experience, and ability to write concisely and completely on excellence in management practice. We wish also to thank the individual volume authors; Diane Asay, project manager; Julie Zinkus, manuscript editor; Karen Jones, managing editor; Lisa Hoberg and Mary Junewick, editorial support; Bill Stanton, design and production management; Susan Swanson, production coordination; Rohani Design, graphics, page design, and composition.

Norman Bodek
Publisher

1

THE NATURE OF LEADERSHIP

What will all of the management improvement techniques, teams, quality, or process improvements amount to in the absence of effective leadership? Nothing.

Specific techniques can be powerful and produce great results only if strong and effective leadership promotes them. More improvement efforts suffer from poor leadership than from poor techniques. Most failures to change are failures of leadership, rather than tools and techniques.

What is effective leadership?

History shows us hundreds of examples of leadership gaining advantage over superior material force. Perhaps there is no better example than the contrasting leadership of the British fleet and the combined French and Spanish fleets of Napoleon at Trafalgar in 1805, a battle that determined competitive advantage, the dominance of the sea, for 100 years.

In force the fleets were almost equal. There were twenty-seven ships in Nelson's fleet and thirty-three in French Admiral Villeneuve's fleet. Neither fleet had the advantage of technology, tools, or equipment. The British fleet, however, had the advantage in method and communication. Nelson had devised a new signaling system that provided more immediate and frequent instructions.

The difference that resulted in catastrophe for the combined French and Spanish fleet by the day's end was in people, not in things. In the British fleet 449 were killed and 1,214 wounded out of 18,000. Among the French and Spanish there was slaughter. Villeneuve's lead ship alone lost 400, and 200 were wounded. Another ship lost 450. The total loss of lives is not known, but it was many thousands. The battle eliminated the threat of Napoleon invading Britain and extending his empire beyond the continent of Europe.

Can a leader make this difference? Villeneuve thought so. When he saw that it was Nelson's flag atop the lead ship, he went below to his cabin and wrote in his diary, "The battle is lost. It is Nelson!"

What was the contrast?

Before the battle, Villeneuve called a war council, for the French and Spanish captains, at which, they exchanged insults and expressed distrust. On the other hand, Nelson and his captains, who were known as the "band of brothers," had repeatedly fought together, knew each other intimately, and trusted each other as brothers.

The combined French and Spanish fleet adhered to the order of battle that had been the standard for the past 100 years. They formed the traditional "line of battle" and expected the enemy to do the same. Nelson, however, innovated and surprised his opponents by sailing perpendicular, running straight at their line. This strategy resulted not in fleet fighting against fleet, but in the disorder and chaos of the broken lines. Now it was ship against ship, captain against captain, crew against crew. Nelson's last and most famous signal to his ships as they sailed toward the French fleet said, "England trusts that every man shall do his duty!" Nelson knew and trusted his captains and men.

Nelson was unquestionably one of the most successful military leaders in history. He was a "tough boss." At

Trafalgar he stood on deck with one arm shot off and the loss of one eye and refused to leave the deck even when the enemy was firing broadside directly across the deck.

While Horatio Nelson was tough on his competition, he was not tough on his own men. There was a camaraderie, affection, and affiliation among them.

As the battle approached, Nelson sent off a mail ship, the last to sail for England before the battle. Nelson then walked the decks of his ship, the *Victory,* and found a despondent common seaman. When asked the reason for his despair, the seaman said that his letter to his family had failed to make the mail ship. Nelson then ordered the recall flag hoisted to bring back the mail ship that was already halfway toward the horizon. This action was ordered for the letter of a solitary seaman. Is this the stuff of which victories are made?

Stories such as those of Nelson's concern for the common seaman portray the bond for which men will die. In the British Navy there was what was called the "Nelson touch." It was simply the bond that existed between Nelson and his men. This loyalty was so strong that when Nelson died, the seamen of the *Victory* insisted that his body remain on board so those who sailed into battle with him could sail his body back home.

Perhaps the most significant advantage at Trafalgar was the skills of the men—officers and enlisted men. The French officer corps had suffered from the excesses of the French Revolution, and many lacked fighting experience. The British officers had all been at sea since they were fourteen-year-old midshipmen, experienced and well-drilled. However, more significantly, the British seamen had been so well-drilled in manning their guns that their rate of fire was twice that of the French and Spanish. Although the British were outgunned, in effect they had almost twice the firepower due to the cycle time of the crews working the guns. The effectiveness of the British broadsides at close range was totally devastating.

It was the effectiveness, the spirit, and the skill of people effectively trained and inspired by their leaders that determined the dominance of the seas for 100 years.

In the warfare of competitive business the conditions are different, but the principles are the same. The ability of leaders to influence their people is key. Captain Horatio Nelson and his men were unified and trusted one another. Nelson innovated and took risks by attempting new tactics and new methods. He delegated and relied on the abilities of his fellow officers. Nelson created advantage through training, human competence, and commitment. In short, he created a quality culture. This demonstrates leadership.

LEADERSHIP: THE BASICS

Leadership is not a complicated topic. It does not, contrary to the belief of some, require great intellect. Examine leaders like Nelson and you will find that they are not distinguished by superior intelligence, academic training, or any physical qualities. However, they do have distinguishing personal qualities—qualities that can be acquired. I believe that the essential qualities of leaders are not hard to understand. They are only hard to implement in one's own life.

The Leader Within

Ernest Hemingway once said that readers possess a "sure-shot automatic crap detector." Well, followers in an organization also possess a "sure-shot automatic crap detector" eternally aimed between the eyes of the leader.

I have come to realize that followers have a sixth sense, an intuitive perception of their leader, perhaps not always accurate, but more often than not, on target. And this sense largely determines their willingness to follow. What they most seek to perceive, their barometer or their measure of the leader, is the gap between actual and stated beliefs; sincerity of commitment; conformance to professed principles; and personal will. They want to trust their leader. They want to know that he or she truly believes in the plotted course. The certainty of this commitment, the reliability of the leader, is the key determinant of followership.

Most of this book addresses what you may *do* to fulfill your role of leadership in the organization. But what you do is the *act,* it is not the *actor,* and to a large extent the act fails if it is incongruous with the actor. I believe that ultimately, it is impossible to act the role of leader. I believe you must become a leader. Acting and doing are very different than being. Consider *becoming* before acting, because if you become a leader, doing follows naturally and is so much more successful.

The Quality of Self-Knowledge

Who am I? Much of our life is devoted to answering this question. As school children we dream of who we might become. In adolescence we worry about who we are and struggle to become like our idols, dreams, or more likely, our parents. As adults we spend the better part of our lives trying to prove that we are competent as professionals and parents.

Those who live troubled lives often perceive themselves in ways that are degrading, that hold them down, that prevent them from fulfilling their potential. It seems to me that to be a leader one must have an expanded sense of self, a belief in the potential self. It is the potential self and understanding that potential that are important in the perceptions of the leader. We are all born with a measure of potential, and it is our duty, I believe, to fulfill, as nearly as possible, that potential. In final judgment it is not merely what we have achieved, but what we have achieved *in relation to our given potential,* that measures our worth.

Leaders understand their potential and measure their own success inwardly, not against others, but against what they have the capacity of achieve. They do not focus on who they are, but on who they *are* capable of *becoming.* To focus on who I *am* is to stand still.

Leaders are often accused of egotism or conceit. Perhaps a degree of egotism is a necessary component of leadership. Perhaps egotism can be constructive, as well as destructive. Constructive egotism is the exalted sense of self expressed to oneself, enabling growth and confident action in the direction of the exalted self. Destructive egotism, which often stems from the lack of self-confidence, leads one individual to make self-congratulatory statements to others so they will view him or her in an exalted manner. Leaders require their own applause more than the applause of others. Applause from others comes cheap. But applause earned from knowing that one is actually succeeding in achieving one's potential, now that is much harder to come by. Leaders focus on their own measures of achievement of potential and are not motivated by external praise. They are freed from rising on their hind legs like puppy dogs wagging their tails, tongues hung out, in hopes for a pat on the head. They know themselves how good or meager their efforts are and how far they have to go before they are ready to be judged for achieving their potential.

The Quality of Purpose

Early in my career I desired to become a good public speaker. One of the best pieces of advice I ever heard in planning a talk was to be sure that what you are saying is important, and to let the audience know why you believe it is important. If it is not important, you surely cannot convince the audience that it is important. Talk only about what you know to be important and talk about it like it is important to the audience.

A one-hour talk is a microcosm of the role of a leader in an organization. Leading is standing in front of an audience. If you plan to lead people, lead them in a direction that is important. Know yourself why it is important. Convey this importance to them. If you know of no important direction or purpose, then get out of the way! What can your organization accomplish that is important? What can it become to make a difference, a significant contribution? Meditate on this potential. Believe in it.

It is characteristic of the human soul to seek meaning or purpose, a cause that is noble and uplifts, a focus of energy and a reason to sacrifice. It is skillful leadership that helps us to connect our lives, our actions, our energies to that purpose; and it is that connection that is the source of energy itself.

Both individuals and institutions who achieve excellence have a deep understanding of their purpose. This understanding of purpose is usually one that is uplifting, that creates within the individual a sense of self-worth, pride, a reason to sacrifice and make a commitment. Many of our business institutions have lost their vitality because they have focused excessively upon financial goals and measures, forgetting their true purpose, to be of service to a customer, to serve the needs of society. The objective of financial results, while necessary to the long-term health of an organization, does not motivate those who perform the work of the organization.

Leaders create human energy by instilling a sense of purpose within their followers. The manager or administrator may direct and control the energy as the driver may steer and control the car. However, the car does not make great progress with no fuel in the tank or fire in the engine. It requires energy to make progress. Human energy is the fire that propels every organization forward toward its goals. And it is leadership that creates this energy.

The mystery of leadership is the focus on a noble purpose, the willingness to call upon others to sacrifice for that which is noble, and therefore, to enoble them. Every leader intuitively understands this process.

The Quality of Creative Dissatisfaction

I have never met an excellent executive who was satisfied. I have met numerous mediocre ones who were. Those who achieve excellence participate in an ongoing struggle with their own competencies. They are active managers of their own learning process.

Change and progress occur as a response to dissatisfaction. A satisfied individual stands still, has no reason to change or grow and more closely approximate his or her potential. Dissatisfaction encourages searching, discovery, change, and growth. Individuals who possess this quality of creative discomfort are a work-in-progress. They are the most valuable resource in an organization. They are able to adjust to change, to benefit from it, and to lead change. The ones who are satisfied are the inertia, the drag, on an organization.

Excellent organizations promote certain types of behavior. They promote the acceptance of responsibility. They promote the most honest and frank feedback between manager and employee (most importantly, from bottom up). They promote high recognition and praise—the payoff for top performance. They promote teamwork because they know that nothing worthwhile gets accomplished unless they focus the power of groups working together on the task. And, they promote the discussion, experimentation, and risks of crazy ideas, ideas that challenge traditional thinking. All of these are corollaries to the pursuit of excellence.

A culture that promotes excellence is also a culture that tolerates mistakes. If a child is to learn and develop, he or she must feel free to explore and to try out new behavior without an overwhelming fear of failure. Criticism or punishment for mistakes destroys learning.

The Quality of Integrity

This is an age of distrust. We have learned that presidents lie. That corporations cheat. That lawyers seek to distort and deceive. That clergymen live dual lives. The effect of distrust is disunity and apathy. If one cannot trust sources of authority, then one is left to wander alone, constantly apprehensive of others. This state is destructive of the individual and detracts from the progress of the organization.

Leadership requires followership, and following is an act of trust. If one person is going to respond and arise to the words or actions of another, the individual must first trust the sincerity, integrity, and truthfulness of the first person. Any seed of doubt or distrust weakens the fabric of order. Any seed of doubt weakens the ability of one individual to influence another. All sound relationships, in marriage, business, in any group, are built on trust.

We defeat trust in subtle ways. We may communicate to influence another in the way we desire without being fully honest. A salesperson may present a product as the best, cheapest, highest quality, most superior product, while knowing otherwise. A manager may fail to tell an employee the whole truth about where he or she stands. An executive may state categorically that no more layoffs are planned, yet within six months, employees are experiencing the trauma of layoffs. Unfortunately, perceptions determine the bond of integrity that holds individuals and organizations together. These perceptions are often unfair. The executive may have told the absolute truth when he or she stated confidently that no more layoffs were planned. It was several months later that they were planned. The perception of deceit is still there. Avoiding these perceptions is no small task in an age in which people have been trained by the media to seek out any hint of falsehood on the part of the leader.

The Quality of Consensus Building

The organizations that succeed in the future will be those that are best at bringing people together, calling upon the input and participation of all. This requires a culture of consensus, not command. In the past a leader commanded his ship in battle, commanded his followers to order, and commanded his will upon his government. Our culture has emerged from a history that has valued the strength of command. All our heroes on television present a strong image of command. It is true that command decision making led to success on the battlefield, and the culture of command is a culture shaped to the necessities of war. We are now entering an era predicated on the necessities of peace-making and unifying.

The institutions of the future will succeed because of the quality of the thinking of their members. Thinking is not something you can command. You cannot stand over someone and yell "think" at them and expect better ideas to emerge. Better ideas emerge when people feel that others will listen to, discuss, appreciate and take their ideas into consideration in an honest and open fashion. This is the style that stimulates creative thinking. And, it is creative thinking that has the highest payoff and is the most productive behavior in today's organization. Past management practices emerged from an age in which manual labor was the focus of management. Consensus-based management practices will succeed in the competition for ideas.

The leaders of the new era will possess the skills and the discipline to work with groups in reaching consensus. The skill of leading a group toward consensus may be called facilitation. Facilitation helps others reach a conclusion. Facilitating is different from commanding or even telling.

Building consensus involves a group of individuals who consider important matters and, with total candor and unity, arrive at a collective wisdom. This, however, requires new skills and personal qualities. Rather than the strength of argument, the strength of asking questions and effective listening distinguish the leader.

The Quality of Unity

This is an age of disunity. It is an age of increasingly divided nations, races, religions, and political parties. It is an age in which individuals promote themselves by highlighting their differences from others. Yet, it is also an age in which these differences are becoming increasingly transparent and irrelevant. This is an age of paradoxes. There are increasing numbers of countries; increasing tribalism. Yet differences are becoming less and less relevant.

At the founding of the United Nations in 1945, it had 51 member states. Today, that number is rapidly approaching 200. Futurist John Naisbitt in his recent book, *Global Paradox,* predicts that in the next century the number will approach 1000, and states that

> . . . *a world of 1000 countries is a metaphor for moving beyond the nation-state. Countries will become more and more irrelevant. The shift will be from 200 to 600 countries, to a million hosts of networks that are all tied together. The people we network with will be more important as the country we happen to operate out of becomes less important."*

The creation of a new world order is not a political philosophy, a position on the left or the right. It is simply a statement of fact, as the movement from agricultural to industrial societies was a material reality. The material of work in this new era is not farmland or industrial equipment, it is knowledge. Knowledge is processed and value is added by bringing information together in an objective manner, without prejudice.

Leaders in the new age will be those who can see the unity, can bring people, ideas, and resources together under a common purpose and understanding. The role of promoting unity—of creating integration out of the disintegration of that which is being cast off—is the key to leadership in the new age.

In the past, those who worked for an institution were neatly divided into two classes: management/labor; salaried/hourly; decision maker/doer. In the past the manager made all the decisions and the worker was just expected to do his or her job as instructed. The organization consisted of two classes of society, much as the military has always consisted of officers and enlisted men.

In the past the distinctions between these two groups made sense and contributed to the organization fulfilling its mission. Today the usefulness of these distinctions is fading fast. Every employee thinks, makes decisions, and is responsible for performance that accompanies those abilities. Every manager works as well as makes decisions. Today adherence to the old principles, in contradiction to the new realities, produces conflict and disunity. It is the major source of ineffectiveness in our secular institutions.

Today we want to involve every individual in the process of management, problem solving, and decision making. This, however, is blocked by the stereotypes and prejudices of the class system that our organizations maintain. Many companies today are gradually moving towards the elimination of these distinctions, and in the future the trappings of the corporate class society will appear as foolish as the trappings of royalty, and the remains of feudal society.

The Quality of Creativity

The creative response is the response of growth. Without it no organization, movement, people, or culture can progress. The creative response is the very sign of vitality and life. When people lose their creativity their defeat is near.

The great historian, Arnold Toynbee, in his *Study of History* concluded that the mechanism of the growth of a civilization was that of challenge and response. He observed that cultures progress as their leaders are able to recognize the challenges the environment presents and issue forth a creative response to that challenge. This leads, in turn, not to a "condition of ease," but rather, to a new and higher-level challenge, that requires a new, creative response. This leads, in turn, to additional challenges and responses. This is the process of growth, until the leaders lose their ability to respond creatively and begin to respond mechanically, pulling the same old lever, harder and faster, although it now fails to meet the new challenges. The leaders and the culture have now achieved a "condition of ease" in which they are unable to respond creatively to new challenges.

Diversity is a source of creativity. To every problem there are many solutions. We must learn to assume that we can take many correct actions in any situation. The better courses of action become evident as we try them. We must learn to think like the experimental scientist, trying out different combinations, and observing their effects without prejudice. We can then repeat and further develop those that are successful. Those that fail require respect as a worthy effort. The better corporations today reward small successes and accept failure as a natural and necessary ingredient in the creative process. These companies, such as 3M, constantly renew and recreate themselves.

The Quality of Will

Bulldog. Determined. Persistent. Relentless. Show me a significant leader and I will show you one of these. Purpose, creativity, and other qualities are the direction and content of the person, but they do not describe the force or strength of the person. The force of will is the muscle with the power to achieve. Two individuals may have the same purpose, but entirely different forces of will.

In working with organizations attempting to change their culture, I believe the ability of the leaders to exert their will is the single most significant factor in success or failure. Some executives only casually desire to change their organizations. Others are fighting for their lives and are willing to overcome all obstacles.

Followers feel the will of their leader, and the energy is passed on, creating a collective will. It is the force of an army marching into battle in which the generals actively seek to convey their confidence and determination to their soldiers because they know that it is this unified effort that will confront and defeat the enemy. So it is in business too.

These are the qualities deep within the person of the leader that determine his or her impact on an organization. Develop these qualities and you are my hero. Develop these qualities and you will change the world.

2

VISION AND VALUES

"Where there is no vision, the people perish."

—Proverbs

Where there is no vision, the business perishes.

All cultures that gain advantage, whether national or corporate, have positive and clearly-defined visions of their future and values that serve to unite and energize their members. The growth of companies such as Apple, Federal Express, Microsoft, McCaw, and others can be associated with the strong vision and clear values of their leaders. Companies in decline have often lost their vision and have become confused about their values.

While vision is the direction, values are the glue. It is common beliefs that hold people together in a society or corporation. The loss of common values and virtues inevitably leads to the decline of nations and corporations. It is the particular job of leaders to clarify and hold people to these values.

Efforts to improve the quality of products and services will produce lasting change if they are viewed as the fulfillment of lasting values and a strategic vision.

Although most companies have some statement of their vision and values, these are often mere words that have little effect on the behavior of managers or employees. The leadership team will do well to review these statements periodically; update them, based on an understanding of quality principles; and assess the degree to which they are operative principles.

Leaders meditate on their vision and values. I use the word "meditate" with some trepidation. The image of a swami sitting on the mountaintop is likely to come to mind. By "meditate," however, I simply mean that the members of the leadership team will do well to think deeply about the implications and potential of their words. When our founding fathers wrote the Constitution, they meditated on the significance of their words. They discussed and fully considered their implications. It is because of the depth of their thought that they were able to construct the framework of a great nation.

The first task of leadership is to create a statement of Vision and Values for the organization. Involve others in the creation. Listen and learn from voices inside the organization and outside. Be sensitively aware of the organization's capability, and of the interest and needs of customers, employees, suppliers, and other company constituencies. Perceive opportunities and obstacles. Create a Vision and Values statement that excites and motivates company people to great achievement. Write it down. Communicate. Listen. Explain. Make vision and values the guiding star for everything the organization does. Clarify and communicate vision and values in all top management behavior.

Vision and values are the starting points for success today and for leading the organization to its intended future. All else flows from vision and values: goals and performance measures, strategy, organization design, action planning, and the implementation actions and continuous improvement that make the vision a reality, with all organization members living and working exemplars of the values. The flow modeled in Figure 1 can be applied at all management levels throughout the company.

When we look at company histories, we see that the founders possessed a vision. An idea that was exciting and unique—often one that others thought impossible to achieve. An idea that eventually mobilized others and created a successful company. It is the role of today's leaders to develop the idea, the vision of the future. Vision stimulates the energy and creativity of the entire organization.

When leaders have a strong sense of purpose, they stay close to the work that leads to relevant decision making and the ability to motivate employees. Employees develop self-worth when they feel connected to business purpose. If they are viewed as "head count" or a business cost, their personal worth is not recognized and their contribution diminished. This is a prescription for loss of creativity and motivation. This motivation will not be regained with some minor manipulation of the compensation system. It will only be regained when *management* itself regains its creativity, its sense of purpose, and when it again develops genuine affection for productive work and productive workers. Management must become leadership committed to vision and values.

In the corporation, the internal power is the creativity of people, the strength of social purpose, the development of competence, and the ability of its members to act with unified and determined effort. The external power of the corporation is its ability to capture and hold market territory, to dominate the competition, and to strengthen its material resources. Both are nurtured and guided by vision, by values and by leadership—at all levels.

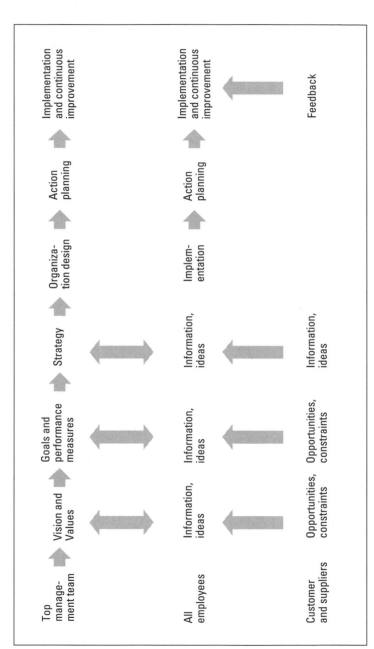

Figure 1. Vision and Values are the Starting Points for All Company Actions

VISION AND VALUES: THE HEART AND MIND

Intuitively, all great leaders understand that their power builds on the vision they share with their followers. When President John F. Kennedy called on people to "ask not what your country can do for you, but what you can do for your country," he was calling for sacrifice toward a common vision.

The vision and values of a company are often captured in simple phrases. At Delta Airlines it is the "Delta family feeling." At Dun & Bradstreet, "customer focus." At Honda Manufacturing it is "the Honda way" and "the racing spirit." Simple statements all. Yet behind those statements are legends, emotions, and subtleties that affect the decisions of employees every day. The slogans are a shorthand way of expressing the company's vision, and it is that vision that gives these companies their competitive advantage.

Before a company can succeed, it must build a foundation that allows for creative energy, dedication, and sacrificial effort, all stemming from a vision of the future.

How can a leader create a unifying vision throughout the company? Through four specific actions:

1. **Develop a Vision Statement.** The organization's leaders must agree on what the company is and should become. This shared vision is the common religion, ethic, and guide to the organization's future. In an emerging company the management team may not have the maturity to develop such a vision. In that case the leader must declare it. This statement should include both the external vision (future markets, products, or services) and the internal culture (values).

2. **Sell the Vision.** A written statement printed in the corporate newsletter, read at the annu-

al conference, or pasted on the wall does not sell. The leadership must market the vision and present it over and over again, like an advertising campaign introducing a new product. Selling the vision is never a one-time thing; it requires continual communication.

Employees do listen. Unfortunately, they often hear too well. The executive who promotes an idea in one speech, but forgets it in the next encourages employees to forget, too. The senior executives should refer to the vision in literally every talk they give to managers and employees. Constant reminders and restatement of the vision is essential if it is to become part of the culture. And actions speak more convincingly than words. Leaders work and walk exactly the way they talk.

3. **Make the Vision an active reference point.** When managers make decisions, they should refer to the Vision Statement and ask whether their decision furthers or detracts from the vision. For example, your vision may include the idea that every employee must be involved in making decisions and accept responsibility for his or her work. You are now considering a training program for new employees. Does the program help employees make decisions about their own work?

Ask yourself this question every time: Is this decision consistent with the company's vision? If it isn't, don't make it.

4. **Praise and publicize models.** Values become clear when behavior consistent with those values is praised and publicized. Write down the two, three, or four key values that are important in your company. In your last talk to managers or employees, did you talk about staff members

who exhibited those values? If you don't praise people for living up to the company's values, they will not assume those values are important. When executives of 3M speak to employees, they almost always refer to internal examples of innovation. When David Kearns was CEO of Xerox, he always talked about the importance of quality improvement and education. When Alexander the Great spoke to his troops, he always spoke of bravery and sacrifice in battle. Do you stress what is important?

3

ENTHUSIASM FOR CUSTOMERS

Revenue comes from customers. Profit comes from customers. The first task of every business is to create and keep customers. Successful companies focus everything they do on satisfying customer expectations, searching always for still better ways to do this. Leaders use vision and values to build market success.

CURRENT MARKET

Your organization is successful because it meets the requirements of your market. This success is the result of current capabilities.

To define future market requirements, begin by understanding how your business is currently positioned in the marketplace and your current strengths and weaknesses.

In many companies there are walls between the marketing organization, product development, and production. The higher or thicker these walls, the more likely your organization is producing products or services that do not meet market requirements. You must remove these walls to create connections between those selling, developing, and producing. You will want to involve people from all of these functions, as well as customers, in the process of defining both current and future market requirements.

Quality improvement efforts traditionally focus on process improvement to meet customer requirements. This understanding of quality has two limitations. The first is the focus on the present rather than the future. The second is the limited understanding of customer requirements. Providing net value to customers is a more complete description of the transaction.

Wal-Mart assigns a full-time employee to greet customers and assist them with a shopping basket. From a short-term financial point of view it would be impossible to justify this cost. This cost is also not justified from a traditional quality perspective. Customers are not asking for this service. If asked their requirements, few customers would suggest this pleasantry. It is, however, an element of net customer value. It is a benefit that weighs against costs.

DuPont, Corning, and other companies invest heavily in research and development to develop products that are not within the imagination of their customers. This research strategy, while not an element of current customer requirements, is an important strategic system that contributes to customer value.

Federal Express developed the technical capabilities to let their customers know where a package is at all times and when and to whom it is delivered. This is possible only because every facility and every truck has a computerized bar-coding system. This capability adds value for customers by providing almost instant information. Only the development of a new capability in their core process could provide this advantage.

Defining what customers currently value is not easy. It is even more difficult to determine how their values, tastes, preferences, and expectations are changing. If you can image your own preferences in food, communication, computing, or automobiles five years ago, you can see the changes that may occur in the next five years. Systems such as those of Federal Express are not short-term responses to customer demands, but rather the result of strategic efforts to develop capabilities to match anticipated value requirements of customers.

Net value is the relationship between total benefits of a product or service and total costs. *Value is increased by increasing benefits and reducing costs.* Value can often be increased by spending to improve the core process and reducing expenditures in nonessential processes. Process owners can continually improve the value-added of a process by constantly studying the process.

Processes involve both monetary and nonmonetary costs. The nonmonetary costs of doing business with your firm may be ignored because they do not appear on a financial statement. However every sales person knows that price is only one of many reasons why a sale may be made. Time that customers spend waiting on the phone

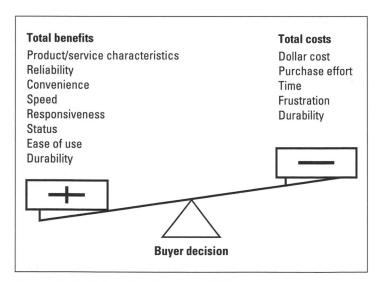

Figure 2. Defining Net Customer Value

Exercise: Define Net Customer Value

Benefit Analysis:	**Cost Analysis:**
List all the benefits desired by your customers. Why are you chosen over competitors?	What are the elements of cost associated with acquiring or using your products or services? Include both tangible and intangible costs.

Rank Order	Rank Order

Computing Value and Costs: This is not meant to be a precise analysis. It is meant to be an exercise to help you define net value as viewed by customers.

Imagine that you are a customer for your product or service, and imagine all the things that you would like to receive from your product or service. Rank the order of importance of those features. Now imagine all the things that may be difficulties, inconveniences, sacrifices, or regrets when a customer buys your product or service. List those as costs. Rank the order of these.

You now have your customer's perception of your benefits and costs. It is critical to point out the companies often misjudge these costs and benefits. For example they are likely to think that the tangible, technical, or mechanical features are the most important. However when customers are asked, they are more likely to rank benefits such as timely delivery, friendly service, attractive colors, etc. For this reason it is critical that your customers participate in this process.

Now do the same for your best competitor. Imagine a customer of this best competitor. How would the customer evaluate the benefits and costs of his product or service?

Now ask the question: which are the most critical benefits and costs to improve? What must we be capable of doing or delivering to meet the customer's needs? What improvement would give us the greatest competitive advantage?

Figure 3. Exercise

is a cost for which they have low tolerance. Another cost is delay or confusion caused by excessively complex processes. Identifying these costs is perhaps the most important component of computing net customer value. Leaders assure that total benefits outweigh total costs.

The greatest experts on total costs and benefits are the customers themselves. Companies must ask customers what they value. Employees who communicate directly with customers are the second greatest experts in what customers value. These two groups must be surveyed to define net value.

While benefits are most often the result of product or service characteristics, costs are more often the result of poor processes. One advantage in analyzing costs and benefits is that it leads to the identification of critical organizational processes that need improvement. For example, a major telephone company required an average of several weeks to install phones in a new office. The quality of the phone and the quality of the phone service were excellent. However, the cost of waiting several weeks often drove customers to the competition. This poor cycle time was a cost that clearly was the result of badly designed work processes and organizational systems.

CURRENT CAPABILITIES

Capabilities include work processes, equipment, physical assets, and human capabilities (see Figure 4). Technical systems are the systems that define how we get the work done. Producing a profit-and-loss statement is an output of a work process in the accounting department. If that work is completed with only the assistance of a mechanical adding machine, it may be capable of delivery thirty days after the end of the month. If a computer and accounting software are purchased, the system may now be capable of delivering the report by the tenth day of the month. This is improved technical capability.

What are the technical capabilities of your core work processes? How do these create distinguishing characteristics that give you or your competitors an advantage? What are the human capabilities?

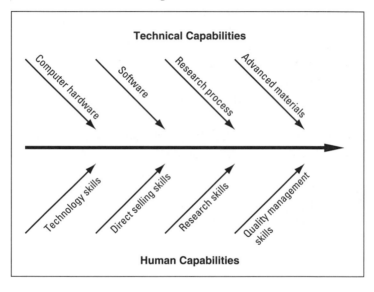

Figure 4. Capabilities

Once you determine your customer's criteria for net value, you can then determine how well your current capabilities meet those requirements and take any needed corrective actions.

FUTURE MARKET REQUIREMENTS

By defining the current net value you provide to your customers, you have gathered a great deal of input to help you predict what customers will value in the future.

The only certainty about future customer value is that it will differ from what it is today. A few trends are predictable for the next ten years.

SPEED

We have become a nation of speed junkies, and our infatuation with fast delivery, fast service, and fast response is a cultural characteristic that no one industry can control. It is related to our education in front of the television with a magic control switch in our hand and many channels to choose among. It is related to our highways, computers, and telephone access to anything. Your business will not escape the upward spiral of speed.

PERSONALIZATION

Retailing and other businesses are becoming increasingly flexible, which allows them to respond to highly individualistic customer tastes. Examine the watch selection at the jewelry counter. There are hundreds with a mind boggling array of features. You can buy clothes of any color with any logo and in any size. One-size-fits-all is dead!

DATA, DATA, DATA

We are a culture of data junkies. CNN gives us the news constantly. Homes have dedicated weather radios. Turn on the television and you receive the NOAA weather report instantly. Stock and mutual fund reports are available each morning or each evening and can be received on your personal computer from a database. Companies provide television monitors throughout the company. Sometimes companies use satellite communication, which provides daily or even hourly reports on company news and results to their headquarters. We want all of the information available now.

Exercise: Future Net Value

Future Total Benefits: What benefits will be desired three to five years from now by your key customers or markets? Which of the present benefits will increase in value? Which will decrease in value?

_____

_____

_____

_____

_____

_____

_____

_____

Future Total Costs: Which of the current costs will increase in the future? Which costs will experience greater competition through lowered costs among competitors? Which cost will increase? In which area of costs do you expect customers to have the greatest demands for reduction? Be sure to consider non-monetary costs such as time, effort, etc.

_____

_____

_____

_____

_____

_____

_____

_____

_____

_____

_____

_____

_____

_____

_____

Figure 5. Exercise: Future Net Value

QUALITY

Japanese cars are only the tip of the iceberg. The population has become highly sophisticated in its expectations of quality. They not only know it when they see it; they read comparative reports analyzing quality results and have the information to demand the facts on quality from sellers. Customer demands never go backwards. They only become increasingly demanding. No matter what your business, you can be assured that you will face a more sophisticated customer in the future.

GUARANTEE IT!

Wal-Mart will take it back if you are not satisfied. Domino's Pizza promises you do not have to pay if you are not satisfied. Even some books offer the promise of your money back if your expectations are not met. Customers increasingly expect that you will stand by your product or service.

You can probably identify other general trends. Given these and given your strategic assumptions, what will be the benefits your customers demand in the future? What will be the possible costs?

Figure 5 is a work sheet to develop a definition of future net customer value.

FINDING FUTURE CUSTOMERS

Leaders consider the drivers that will change market conditions. Then they do the hardest thing of all. They imagine the characteristics they could create that would result in increased business in the future. This is a creative task. It is best done with groups who engage in true brainstorming. The best process is to have a series of sessions with employees, customers, and suppliers who collectively share their thinking about the future. As a starting point, complete the following sentences:

In the future when customers think of our company, we want them to think of_____

_____

_____

_____

_____

_____

In the future the majority of customers will buy from us because _____

_____

_____

_____

_____

_____

The one thing that we will do better than anyone else will be _____

_____

_____

_____

_____

_____

_____

As future customers come into view, the task of the leader is to develop the capabilities of the organization to create and keep those customers. Figure 6 illustrates this process.

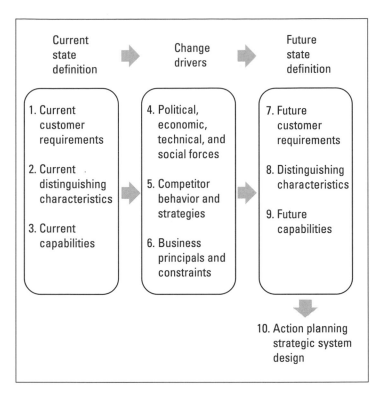

Figure 6. Leadership Map

4

TEAMWORK AND PROBLEM SOLVING—AT ALL LEVELS

The burden of leadership is to be the example—to lead. Being the example is the first and most powerful meaning of leadership. Leaders who asks others to follow the course that they themselves are unwilling to follow are not leaders at all.

How many times have we seen management support a culture change below them, yet fail completely to embrace the practices themselves? This inevitably results in failure.

At Delta Airlines the nine senior executives meet each Monday morning to share decisions and seek each other's help and consultation. The "Delta family feeling" is not a program imposed from the top on "those who need it" below. Rather, it is a belief system that is integrated from top to bottom.

At three major oil companies, we at the Miller Howard Consulting Group implemented total team systems throughout the entire exploration and production organizations. In all three cases we trained and coached the most senior team of managers to practice the teamwork, customer focus, and process improvement that they had prescribed for the entire organization. In all three cases, lower-level employees were very sensitive to the behavior of the senior managers, and the changes in their practices established the credibility of the entire process.

The senior team must be willing to work on their own practice of effective team decision making, customer focus, process improvement, and other management practices if they expect these to become the norm throughout the organization.

One of the most common reasons for failure is that senior managers accept the new practices intellectually, but not in their hearts, their guts, or their habits. They have not internalized the concepts because they have not practiced or seen their effect first-hand or witnessed their results. Their faith has not been confirmed by deeds, and it is only through deeds that their faith becomes real. Without this strength, with the first pressures they quickly resort, like straws in the wind, to their old style.

The solution to this is for the senior leadership group to train in the practices of team management. This training should include defining the processes that add value; defining their customers, suppliers, and requirements; defining feedback loops; agreeing on which decisions will be team responsibilities; defining how and when to hold team meetings; learning the skills of team facilitation and team problem solving; and most importantly, developing clear action plans and accountability.

An immediate reaction may be that this sounds like a lot of extra work. However, this *is* their work. It is not "extra" work. Making effective decisions, serving customers well, etc., *is* the substance of their work. Effective teamwork and a focus on quality should improve their work.

Many high-level management teams view their function as reviewing the work of other people and passing judgment on this work and the results. They have become a court of judges, not a team of players or problem solvers. It is rather easy to stand aloof and judge. It is entirely a different matter to solve problems. Solving problems requires analysis of data, applying intellect to the process, and thinking creatively about solutions. It is important that your own team participates in the management process by solving problems, not simply judging the work of others.

It is important that the managers of each organizational unit feel ownership and responsibility for the organization they lead. Therefore, the best case is for those managers to redesign their own organization consistent with the new assumptions of what we refer to as *team management*. What are the assumptions of team management?

- Workers want to accept responsibility for the performance of their work teams, and given the necessary training, information, and organization, will execute that responsibility constructively.

- The less management required to get the job done, the better. Fewer layers of management allow workers to accept more responsibility, increase innovation and response time, improve communication, and reduce costs.

- The first line manager can be trained to lead a team, or several teams more effectively than he or she can direct and control individual performance. In team management, the first line manager becomes a facilitator, advisor, and trainer.

- Everyone in the organization is a member of a performance team with specific and measurable responsibilities. Teams function best when they closely watch their "score" and strive to break "records" for excellent performance.

- Every performance team is led by a manager, although employee members may facilitate the teams.

- Teams interlock, with the leader of each team serving on a team of leaders led by a second-level manager (who also serves on a team at that level). The team process can extend to the CEO and the top executive team. Team management is most effective when it is a total process of management at every level of the organization.

- Teams have access to all data on their performance. They review that performance at set intervals (usually weekly), set objectives for performance, problem-solve their performance, and develop action plans for improvement.

- The more mature an employee team (like an individual) the more responsibility that team can accept. Teams must be gradually nurtured toward accepting responsibility for their self-management.

- Managers must adopt significantly new skills and behavior in order to lead teams. The task of management must be redefined, the organization and systems changed, and most importantly, managers trained and coached in the new leadership behavior.

In high performance organizations, managers at every level of the organization view themselves as team leaders who are skilled at leading group problem-solving sessions that maximize the collaboration across units of the organization. These meetings provide a forum that educates these managers in the problems and concerns of other departments.

The nine most senior managers of Delta Airlines constitute what I would describe as a leadership team. Every Monday morning they meet to discuss major issues facing the company, to report any major events in each of their areas, and to get advice from other team members. It is this last feature that is most important. It is this willingness to seek advice that genuinely makes this a high-performance company.

The culture of Delta Airlines is not the result of any short-term effort or any specific program. It is the result of consistent management practices, beliefs, and behavior, from top to bottom. The "Delta family feeling" begins with the family feeling among the nine senior executives who have the maturity to talk together as adults, who look to learn from each other. It is this feeling of respect and maturity that provides the basis for teamwork and problem solving at all levels.

5

LEADERS MAKE CHANGE HAPPEN

Peter Drucker tells us the corporation exists for two purposes: innovation (of product) and marketing.[1] When it fails at the first, it will be unable to succeed at the second. It is the nature of bureaucracy to stifle creativity. It is up to the leaders of the organization to free that creativity by pointing out the gap between where we are today and where we could be tomorrow. The members of the organization must have a clear vision of the future. A burning desire to accomplish a goal is the only way to break bureaucratic constraints. What is worth getting excited about, losing sleep over, sacrificing for? Why will you be proud to have served this company? You, the leader, must be able to answer these questions.

Many corporate leaders fail to understand that the real business of the corporation is innovation. In today's rapidly changing, highly competitive business environment, the corporation must constantly reinvent itself—its products, services, and marketing—in order to grow. The challenges of creating new products, services, and marketing methods—as well as controlling costs and quality—are all internal ones.

These challenges require creativity. Creative responses are always, by definition, *different*. Administrators may think they can manage creativity, or solve the "creativity problem" by assigning it to a specific department and giving it a budget. How much money will the company allocate to research and development, and what will the return be on that investment? But this is using rational faculties to solve a nonrational problem. This approach to the problem *is* the problem.

Leaders work differently. Their task is to build a total culture that supports creativity. Not only must it tolerate a degree of disorder, but it must also foment an atmosphere of adolescent enthusiasm. A creativity culture emphasizes achieving victories rather than control, counting, and recording.

Peter Drucker argues that innovation, creating the future, is

> . . . *capable of being presented as a discipline, capable of being learned, capable of being practiced. Entrepreneurs need to search purposefully for the source of innovation, the changes and their symptoms that indicate opportunities for successful innovation.*[2]

Drucker is right. In particular, mature companies can stimulate, encourage, and reward the process of innovation. Throughout the company, management must draw out employees who exhibit visionary qualities. To pave the way for innovation, we must create systems that open channels for ideas and energy that might otherwise be blocked. A system for stimulating creativity will provide an ongoing forum where engineers or chemists or architects can discuss advances and applications of their technology.

Social and monetary rewards for employees who propose new product applications not only set a precedent, but spur new ideas. Systematic training of managers in team leadership skills enables managers and employees to engage in a free flow of ideas. Systems must be enabling systems, rather than systems that control.

From the research organizations of Bell Labs, IBM, and the large pharmaceutical companies, thousands of innovations not only have dramatically enhanced their companies' progress, but also have changed the world. Within these companies, creative people are not only tolerated, but encouraged. Johnson & Johnson and 3M have done a particularly good job of fostering internal entrepreneurship and rewarding people who develop new products. Such farsighted practices permit change agents and entrepreneurs to survive in the mature corporation.

RESPONDING TO THE ENVIRONMENT

No culture is an island. The corporation suffers constant pounding from the waves of technological change, political and economic swings, and shifting social norms. It is useless to view the managers of a corporation as the sole determinants of their corporate culture when forces far beyond their control can blow away their best plans and intentions.

Technological changes are forcing shifts in the culture of virtually every corporation. The company president carries a laptop computer and, from his hotel at night, taps into the company computer to receive not only his messages, but the daily reports from each of his twenty-six manufacturing plants. He then plots a graph so he can compare performance over the last twelve months. Previously, the president received this kind of data once a quarter, and dozens of highly paid managers spent days or weeks preparing it. Now he receives it instantly in his hotel room a thousand miles away.

The day is rapidly approaching when every employee will directly access and input information into the computer and will have immediate access to all significant information. What changes will this produce?

It will produce efficient management: fewer managers will handle more data. With more immediate information, employees at every level will be better able to solve problems. The improved flow of information will increase creativity and improve problem solving.

Technology will also affect the marketplace in which the company competes. Technology is changing so rapidly that increasing numbers of companies will be caught in technological market traps.

The political environment continually produces shocks to the corporation. Equal Employment Opportunity laws, liability laws, tax changes, the defense budget, and industry deregulation are all political decisions that affect the beliefs and behavior of employees.

The social environment exerts control both through market forces and the pool from which employees are drawn. Every consumer marketing organization constantly has its ear to the ground trying to sense changes in the social environment that may alter buying patterns.

A company's culture, while largely controlled by management, cannot be divorced from external influences of technology, the economy, politics, and the social environment. Management cannot change these forces, but it must respond to them. In the past, the culture of an organization was viewed as something immovable. Today, the culture of every corporation is constantly changing, responding to the challenge of foreign competition and new market conditions.

This is the most exciting and, I believe, most desirable time ever to be managing in a corporation. Why? Because when dynamic conditions exist, competitive advantage can be quickly gained or lost. This is a time when you can influence the culture and direction of your organization. An inert object is difficult to direct. An object in motion changes direction with just slight pressure to one side or the other.

There is one final reason why this is the most desirable time to be a corporate manager. When historians look back on the last quarter of the twentieth century, they will see it represented the most revolutionary change in mankind's conduct of business. It will be seen as a period of collective synergy and interdependence. For thousands of years it has been assumed that to achieve spiritual progress, one had to be detached from the pursuit of the material. The holy men of the past went to the desert to demonstrate their detachment from the material. The merchant trading in the bazaar and the lender of money was assumed to be morally corrupt. Perhaps this was true in the past. But we are entering a day in which all things are made new, and among them will be the relationship between the material and spiritual.

The task that confronts every leader in every organization is to create a culture that successfully pursues the creation of wealth, but in a manner that enhances the spiritual progress of all its members.

PRIORITIZING CAPABILITY IMPROVEMENTS

To make needed changed happen, capabilities, too, must change. The improvement in strategic systems is a *leadership responsibility* of the CEO and his or her team of managers, each of whom should be responsible for leading a strategic subsystem. Figure 7 illustrates the relationship between company subsystems and the current and future capabilities of these subsystems.

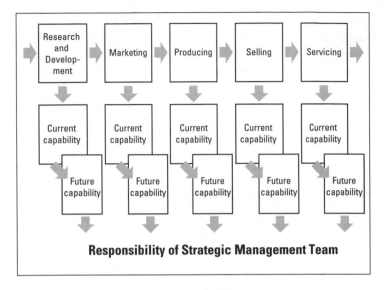

Figure 7. Strategic Systems Capability

6

PERFORMANCE RESULTS—THE MEASURE OF LEADERSHIP

Leaders translate beliefs into action. After all, it is action that produces results. Vision and Values state the goals of leadership. These 5 S's provide the method:

- Structure

- Systems

- Skills

- Style

- Symbols

STRUCTURE

I began my career working as a counselor in the North Carolina Department of Corrections. Perhaps nowhere is the power of an organization's structure more obvious than in a prison.

In the early 1970s a university study was designed to determine the effects of prison structure on human behavior. A mock prison was devised, and twenty graduate students in psychology, products of a humanistic liberal education, were randomly divided into two groups: inmates and guards. For ten days, twenty-four hours a day, the students lived the lives of inmates and guards.

Unfortunately, the experiment had to end early. Why? Because after only a few days the inmates started plotting against the guards and taunting them. The guards, responding out of frustration, began physically abusing the inmates. After the experiment was called off, the students and professor sat together to talk about their experience. None of them could understand their own behavior. The environment, role, and structure of this mock prison had exerted an influence that overcame the education and humanistic values of these students. The roles and structure of corporations accomplish the same.

Just as the roles defined by the prison structure influenced the behavior of the psychology students, the structure of management-union, supervisor-worker, and salaried-hourly relationships constantly influence the thinking and behavior of employees.

Amoco and Shell Oil Companies, Chrysler, Eastman Chemicals, and dozens of other companies have restructured their organizations around newly defined work processes and with a new cultural vision. In each case, the companies reduced layers of management by moving decision making into the work force. The Dana Corporation has one plant that has a shift with only one manager for over 250 employees. Obviously the assumptions about organizational structure are significantly different from those in a traditional organization. The decision-making workforce represents a new vision of the role of employees.

Recently the average span of control—that is, the number of employees reporting to a manager—at the first level of U.S. manufacturing companies was seven, *exactly what it was one hundred years ago*. It is currently closer to 12.

But, why not 1-to-30, or 50? The manager might reply, "How can I control the work of fifty employees?"

Perhaps the manager can't. But employees can control their own work.

Employees aren't the greatest cause of corporate inefficiency. Managers are—by assuming they must "control" employees, check every action, and control the checkers with more checkers. Until recently, Ford had sixteen layers, compared with six at Toyota, yet Ford's quality and employee efficiency were worse, a fact that Ford recognized. The company has now substantially reduced the layers of management and increased spans of control by giving employees more say in their jobs. The result has been a substantial improvement in both output per employee and quality.

Dana Corporation revolutionized their culture when they reduced management layers from fifteen to five. Xerox has reduced layers in its manufacturing and service organizations, while at the same time increasing market share, quality, and customer service ratings. There is more and more evidence that the greater the number of management layers, the less efficient is employee productivity. In other words, there is an inverse relationship between the amount of management control and the resulting quality in either product or service.

The structure of the organization is an obvious way of conveying what management believes.

ACTION PLANS TO IMPROVE STRUCTURE

Redesign the Organization

Institute a planning process by which your managers and employees may redesign the organization. A steering committee of senior managers should write a charter to define the principles, or vision, upon which to build the structure. Create design teams made up of line managers and employees. Train them and lead them through a process where they consider work flow and all matters that relate to the organization. Their task is to create the ideal future structure. They then present their recommendations to the steering committee for approval.

Track Spans of Control

I am amazed how few managers are aware of the numbers of layers of management and spans of control they have created. Once you understand the relationship between competitive advantage and the structure of the organization, it makes sense to keep precise data on that structure, especially the numbers of layers and spans of control.

There can be no simple rules for the number of layers or the span of control. These will vary with the work. Obviously, a factory in which repetitive work is the norm can have larger work units than a high-tech engineering department in which first-level managers are heavily involved in problem solving. However, a study of competitors can provide direction and the basis for quantifiable goals. DuPont, for example, studied competing chemical plants in the United States, Europe, and Japan before establishing the goal of substantially increasing their spans of control. This effort produced substantial saving without hindering operational effectiveness.

Define the Existing Organization as Teams

You may not be prepared to totally redesign your organization. Still, you can reduce management layers and give employees more say in their jobs. Here's one way: Rather than thinking about your organization chart as a series of one-on-one reporting relationships, think of it as a series of interlocking triangles composed of managers and employees working in teams, where each team is led by a senior person who is a member of the team above.

This team organization requires no revolution in structure—only changes in skills and style. It implies that the leader of each team is the facilitator of problem solving and decision making within the group. It assumes managers will encourage team members to take responsibility for their own performance. If the manager begins to act more as a team member, the members will begin to act more as managers. Over time this thinking reduces the need to increase structure and reduces alienation. This process has been successful at Tennessee Eastman, Metropolitan Life Insurance Company, Southwestern Bell, and other companies.

SYSTEMS

The flow of information, performance appraisal, and systems of promotion and compensation are among the dozens of systems that allow the organization to maintain efficiency and sanity. Without systems, every event would be treated as unique and require a separate judgment. Chaos could result.

But exactly what "order" is it that the systems are maintaining? The information flow of the military organization causes all information to flow upward to the commanding officer, with little, if any, horizontal flow. That makes sense on the battlefield, where the commanding officers make the decisions.

But the more an organization grows, the more management must delegate the decision-making process. The high performance organization is highly collaborative with managers involved in team decisions at every level.

This requires immediate performance feedback and scorekeeping by each team (see Figure 8).

The systems of compensation and benefits in most organizations are based on differentiated vertical classes.

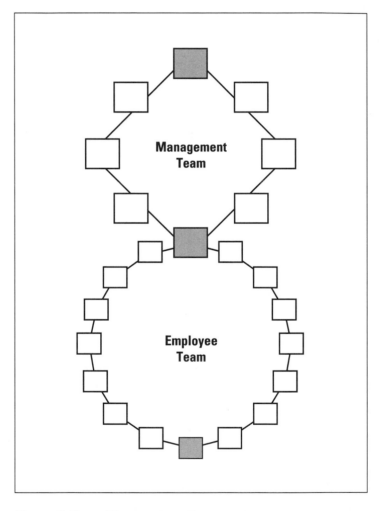

Figure 8. Team Management Structure

Senior managers receive stock options and lower-level employees don't. Why? Obviously we value managers at higher levels more than employees, and we want people to strive to move "upward." But why not offer stock options for employees who progress laterally, people who improve their skills or improve performance within one layer of the organization? Don't we value this, too?

Similarly, profit sharing was designed for the upper classes of our minisociety on the assumption that profits stem from decisions that managers make and not from employees who just follow orders. Is that assumption still true? Such a system teaches employees that they are not responsible for producing earnings. Therefore, why should they try to improve margins? Is that the message we want to send?

Every system in the company is based, in some measure, on values and visions of the organization. If the organization's performance is to be improved, the systems will have to be realigned based on our values and visions of today and tomorrow.

ACTION PLANS
TO IMPROVE SYSTEMS

There are dozens of strategies for improving the systems that affect performance. However, I have found the following to have the greatest impact in terms of reducing bureaucracy and inertia and maximizing employee involvement.

Define and Track Performance for Every Team

If the organization is viewed as a series of interlocking teams, each team must have the information that allows it to accept responsibility for its performance. Each team should meet on a regular basis to discuss and review how performance may be improved. In a manufacturing organization employee teams should meet at least weekly, some even meet once every day. Management teams at lower levels should meet weekly, higher levels less often.

Implement Statistical Process Control

The Japanese success story has been explained in many ways. One technique, however, perhaps more than any other, can be credited for their superior quality. Statistical process control was introduced to the Japanese by W. Edwards Deming. Statistical process control, or SPC, provides continuous monitoring of statistical variation in quality and graphic plotting of variability of products and services on "control charts" and establishes the basis for employee problem solving, or continuous improvement. This method requires considerable training and creates a very different philosophy about the management of performance. It shifts from blaming and controlling to analyzing and correcting.

Implement Performance Management Methods

Performance management, like SPC, teaches managers to be more systematic in their attempts to improve performance. This method is based on the use of behavioral psychology, particularly the principles of positive reinforcement, behavior shaping, and feedback. Each manager should develop action plans to improve performance and systematically reward those improvements.

Redesign the Total System

The most comprehensive way to address the question of whether present systems are helping to create synergy is to redesign the entire organization. The redesign calls for putting aside all systems and creating new ones as the new design requires. This is a *reengineering* approach. It has the advantage of potentially eliminating systems that are viewed as sacred cows.

In a comprehensive redesign process at Moody's Investor Services, publishers of *Moody's Manuals,* the design teams were comprised of first-level employees and managers. They created a total system for judging skills and rewarding performance based on training, competency, and promotions. The design teams expected the steering committee to reject their compensation plan because it included raises for most employees. They justified these raises on the increased levels of responsibility and skill required to perform the new jobs they created as part of the redesign. To their surprise, the steering committee, which included the division human resources manger, accepted their proposal and even considered the raises conservative. The redesign resulted in a 30 percent increase in productivity and the creation of several new products that created new revenues.

SKILLS

As companies mature, skills become more specialized. Many of our modern organizations suffer from overspecialization. This illness is common both at the top and the bottom. Executives at the top may know only finance and not understand production or marketing. At the bottom, the work is so fragmented that workers can't feel any pride in the final product.

In the mature corporation, it is also likely there will be a shift from the functional skills of product innovation, producing, and selling to the support skills of financing, planning, and personnel. The bulk of American industry in recent years has suffered from a shift in emphasis from the primary skills to support skills.

ACTION PLANS TO IMPROVE SKILLS

Most senior executives are so concerned with the financial reports of yesterday's performance that they give almost no attention to developing the potential of their employees—the people upon whom the company's future depends. This is both cause and symptom of the corporation in decline.

Develop an Ethic of Continual Improvement

The best companies believe in continual improvement. For example, we may be the best producer of cellular telephone equipment today, but we know that we must be even better tomorrow, and we are passionately focused on that challenge. Employees have a disciplined pursuit of personal competence—through continuing education—that never ends until the day they retire. Those companies and cultures that are healthy are characterized by continual learning and discovery. Those in decline know all the answers.

Cross-Train at Every Level

An ethic of continual improvement is exemplified not only by providing the best training possible for a specific job, but by ensuring all employees are cross-trained in complementary skills and jobs. This cross-training increases organizational flexibility, improves problem-solving skills, and enhances the self-esteem of all employees.

Celebrate Technical Achievement and Achievers

We reward what is important. We place medals on war heroes and athletes. We have Emmys, Oscars, and Tonys. We have MVPs and Hall of Famers. There is a good chance that you can name last year's winners of some of these awards. But can you name the winner of your company's engineering award? The innovation award? Why can't you name them? The answer is, they are not important! Or so our culture is teaching us.

STYLE

The character of day-to-day interactions among the members of an organization is the organization's style. Although the style of managers is inevitably linked to their skills, it is also tied to the company structure and systems and even the physical environment in which the work takes place.

In a foundry in Monongahela, Pennsylvania, the workers melted scrap iron and poured the molten liquid—with sparks flying—into huge molds to form castings often weighing several tons. The heat of summer, or the cold of the Pennsylvania winter, blows through the large sheds that house the furnaces. This is a loud, dirty, and dangerous place. The men are strong. They stand like soot-covered statues, with blackened muscles and bulging arms, ready to pull, lift, and push the mass that is the product of their work. Their speech is direct, and they will say exactly how they feel with an emotional force that is as honest as their work.

In this foundry there had been a virtual war between management and labor, and more recently within the ranks of the workers themselves. When I first visited this plant, the workers glared at me and each other with distrust and anger.

The corporate climate of manufacturing plants, whether chemical, steel, or coal, in the mountain region of western Pennsylvania and West Virginia was the worst of any in the United States. The fierce sense of independence and antiauthoritarianism, combined with a history of adversarial managers, had produced a self-reinforcing cycle of animosity.

In the Monongahela foundry our consultant was training the managers in how to praise employees and give feedback. The first time one employee was praised for doing a good job, he became so angry that he filed a grievance, claiming the supervisor was making fun of him. Unfortunately, praise was so deviant from the normal style of interaction between managers and workers that the employee completely misinterpreted it. This management style could change only gradually, as the structure and systems gave way to the new culture. After a year of training, the culture changed dramatically as the employees recognized their common interest with managers.

Style has a significant effect on an organization's ability to make effective decisions, motivate employees, and bring about unified action. The style of managers can be clearly seen in the group decision-making process. One manager with whom I worked claimed to be a great advocate of participative decision making. In group meetings he would proclaim loudly that he wanted everyone to speak his mind and that "this is a group decision." But none of his managers ever believed him. When I observed his behavior in a meeting, I found out why. When he stated his opinion he did so with an intimidating tone of voice, one that signaled to everyone in the room that there was only one right decision. His style stifled the participative process.

ACTION PLANS TO IMPROVE STYLE

Sending managers to "charm school" does not improve management style. Management style improves only when it has room to improve and leads to promotions that are tied to improvements in organizational performance. Style characteristics cannot be taught in isolation. They must be taught as a component of a "new way of managing."

Team Leadership Training

Managers must learn the skills of collaborative decision making and leading groups toward consensus. Listening and conflict resolution skills are essential components of such training.

Promote the Company Man (Woman) and the Company

In years past there was much talk about the "company man." Every company with a strong and cohesive culture has some ideal of the company man.

For many years, it was a fact of organizational life that the manager who got promoted at any auto or steel company would be tough in his dealings with people. He talked tough and made tough decisions. Obviously this taught a generation of managers to behave the same way.

In any corporate culture today, those men and women likely to be promoted conform to some stereotypical ideal. What is that ideal? Why not state it openly and with clarity? Why not state that the company's ideal manager will be one who increases the self-esteem of his or her employees?

Continual Appraisal and Feedback.

When a company is young and entrepreneurial, the senior managers will be so close to all the action that formal systems of performance appraisal and feedback won't be necessary. Not so in a mature company. Although it is true that managers should give frequent feedback to reports without the requirement of a system, the truth is they won't. The discipline of a system that requires this feedback is necessary for continuous improvement. Appraisals and feedback should always include the *way* managers get things done, as well as *what* they get done. Style matters. It impacts the commitment, loyalty, and satisfaction of employees. Be certain your appraisal includes an evaluation—plus structured feedback—on management style.

Constant Example by Senior Executives

Why does the chairman of the Dun & Bradstreet Corporation hold informal breakfast meetings with first-level employees every month? Why does he personally visit customers of his twenty-eight business units just to ask them if there is any way in which D&B services could be improved? It is not because he intends to directly affect those employees or customers. This, of course, may happen. But the real purpose is to show thousands of other D&B managers the value of listening to employees and customers. This is the behavior he wants all of his employees to engage in. And rather than just tell them to do it, he has decided to show them. Leaders lead by example. True leaders have always understood that the best way to affect the behavior of others is to serve as an example. This is particularly true in changing management style.

SYMBOLS

We employ all sorts of symbols ritualistically and give little thought to their origin or their impact on behavior. We have separate parking and entrances for managers and employees. Why? To send a message that managers are different from, superior to, and more important than employees. Why do we want to send this message? Mr. Irimajiri, the president of Honda Manufacturing, sits at his desk in Marysville in a large open room with dozens

of others, of every rank, all dressed alike in a white uni-
forms. The reason for this is more symbolic than functional. The message clearly is that everyone at Honda is
valued equally. Honda does not seem to have suffered as
a result of these nontraditional symbols.

Symbols are generally not important by themselves.
Whether the president of Honda has a private office or
not, whether there are separate parking places for employees and managers, has little impact on the bottom line.
But the message those symbols send are important.

7

NINE AXIOMS OF LEADERSHIP

From the discussion of leadership in the first six chapters of this book we can define nine axioms successful leaders, and their organizations, seem to follow to achieve success.

AXIOM 1: SPIRIT

Corporations are both spiritual and material in nature. In their youth, they possess more spiritual than material assets. In decline this reverses.

- **Corollary 1:** It is the function of leaders to instill a unifying, challenging, and rewarding spirit.

- **Corollary 2:** A healthy organization unifies and maintains both spiritual and material assets. Leaders must appreciate the need for both.

- **Corollary 3:** A decline in the spirit of a culture precedes and leads to a decline in material wealth.

AXIOM 2: PURPOSE

The purpose of a business is to create real wealth by serving its constituent groups—customers, stockholders, employees, and the general public.

- **Corollary 1:** A group's performance is a result of common social purpose. It is the function of leadership to instill and reinforce social purpose.

- **Corollary 2:** Emerging cultures possess a clear and unifying social purpose. In decline, that purpose is lost.

- **Corollary 3:** The primary social purpose of a corporation is to serve customers. All employees, at all levels, should know their customers and their needs.

AXIOM 3: CREATIVITY

Business's most important job is to create new and improved products, services, and means of production.

- **Corollary 1:** Leadership must be creative to stimulate creativity.

- **Corollary 2:** Change, youthfulness, and energy are requirements until death.

- **Corollary 3:** Flexibility, challenge, and the free and frank flow of ideas and information are necessary to promote creativity.

AXIOM 4: CHALLENGE AND RESPONSE

The task of leaders is to create or recognize the current challenge, respond creatively, and avoid a condition of ease.

- **Corollary 1:** Effort is the result of perceived challenge and anticipated successful response.

- **Corollary 2:** Reliance on yesterday's successful response in the face of new challenge leads to decline.

- **Corollary 3:** Recognizing and responding to challenges require a culture that is dynamic, never static.

AXIOM 5: PLANNED URGENCY

The urgency to decide and act promptly leads to expansion and advance. Balance prompt action with deliberate planning.

- **Corollary 1:** Planning that results in late action is useless.

- **Corollary 2:** Action that does not serve long-term interests is useless.

- **Corollary 3:** There will always be conflict between promptness and planning.

AXIOM 6: UNITY AND DIVERSITY

Advancing cultures become diverse in character. Leaders must act to unify diverse talents and traits.

- **Corollary 1:** Leaders must actively resist the tendency to attract and promote like personalities and skills.

- **Corollary 2:** Groups attain the highest-quality decisions through consensus. Consensus is most valuable when it represents the collective wisdom of participants with diverse views and experience.

AXIOM 7: SPECIALIZED COMPETENCE

Specialized knowledge and skills must be pursued vigorously. Once obtained, the skills must be integrated.

- **Corollary 1:** Efficient methods are derived from specialized competence; however, specialized competence can lead to inefficient methods.

- **Corollary 2:** The highest technical competence leads to competitive advantage, *if* put to the service of customers, both internal and external.

- **Corollary 3:** Employees at all levels should work in small groups or teams toward a common purpose, as an integrating mechanism.

AXIOM 8: EFFICIENT ADMINISTRATION

As differentiation increases, efficient administration is required to achieve integration and performance.

- **Corollary 1:** The greater the differentiation in an organization, the greater the need for administration.

- **Corollary 2:** The weight of administration tends to grow unless deliberately checked by leadership.

- **Corollary 3:** Unchecked administration inevitably leads to bureaucracy and the decline of creativity and wealth creation.

AXIOM 9: ON-THE-SPOT DECISIONS

Decisions should be made by those on the spot, close to the customer, product, or service. The farther decisions are removed from the point of action, the worse the quality and the higher the cost.

- **Corollary 1:** In the successful company, decision makers are on the spot and in direct contact with customers, products, or services. In decline they are not.

- **Corollary 2:** Command decision making is a sign of a company in stages of immaturity and extreme decay. Consensus is a sign of maturity and health.

- **Corollary 3:** Internal conflict results in increased control. Control produces fear. Fear drives decisions up the organization and drives creativity out.

NOTES

1. Peter Drucker, *Management: Tasks, Responsibilities, Practices* (New York, NY: Harper and Row, 1974): 61.
2. Peter Drucker, *Innovation and Entrepreneurship: Practices and Principles,* (New York: Harper and Row, 1985): 19.

FURTHER READING

1. Steven R. Covey, *Principle Centered Leadership* (New York: Summit Books, 1990). I think this is Covey's best work and as good a piece as you will find on leadership and the importance of principle and purpose.

2. Francis J. Gouillart and James N. Kelly, *Transforming the Organization* (New York: McGraw-Hill, 1995). This recent book, one among dozens on transforming or reengineering the corporation, does a superior job of seeing the organization as a "whole," or organically interrelated.

3. Gary Harnel and C.K. Pralahad, *Competing for the Future* (Boston: Harvard Business School Press, 1994). The business of leaders is largely strategic, and this book does an excellent job of redefining the strategic tasks for business in today's world.

4. Lawrence M. Miller, *Barbarians to Bureaucrats: Corporate Life Cycle Strategies* (New York: Clarkson M. Potter, 1989). Yes, one of my own, which I think does a good job of describing the diversity of leadership roles at different times and circumstances in the life of a company.

5. James Brian Quinn, *Intelligent Enterprise* (New York: Summit Books, 1990.) This book does an excellent job of providing data and the persuasive argument that the requirement of the organization and enterprise are changing in historically significant ways.

ABOUT THE AUTHOR

Lawrence M. Miller began his career by redesigning a prison system, establishing the first free economy behind prison walls, with each inmate having to pay rent, maintain a checking account, and pay for everything he wanted.

He formed his own firm, The Miller Consulting Group, in Atlanta in 1983. His work is directed at rethinking the fundamental system of work and organization, involving every manager and employee, and avoids the creation of "add-on" programs. His efforts typically result in a highly self-managed work force that serves customers and provides feedback to suppliers, internal and external.

His consulting clients have included Shell Oil Company, Corning, Texaco, Tennessee Eastman, Xerox, The Upjohn Company, Harris Corporation, Exxon, and Metropolitan Life.

Mr. Miller is the author of *American Spirit: Visions of a New Corporate Culture; Barbarians to Bureaucrats: Corporate Life Cycle Strategies; Whole System Architecture;* and *Team Management.* He has written for *The New York Times,* and has been the subject of a feature story in *Industry Week.* He has appeared on the *Today Show,* CNN, FNN, and CNBC.

Miller/Howard Consulting Group, Inc., 750 Hammond Drive, Building 12, Suite 200, Atlanta, GA 30328, Telephone: 404-255-6523.

PRAISE FOR THE MANAGEMENT MASTER SERIES

"A rare information resource.... Each book is a gem; each set of six books a basic library.... Handy guides for success in the '90s and the new millennium."

Otis Wolkins
Vice President Quality Services/Marketing
Administration, GTE

"Productivity Press has provided a real service in its *Management Master Series*. These little books fill the huge gap between the 'bites' of oversimplified information found in most business magazines and the full-length books that no one has enough time to read. They have chosen very important topics in quality and found well-known authors who are willing to hold themselves within the 'one plane trip's worth' length limitation. Every serious manager should have a few of these in their reading backlog to help keep up with today's new management challenges."

C. Jackson Grayson, Jr.
Chairman, American Productivity & Quality Center

"The *Management Master Series* takes the Cliffs Notes approach to management ideas, with each monograph a tight 50 pages of remarkably meaty concepts that are defined, dissected, and contextualized for easy digestion."

Industry Week

"A concise overview of the critical success factors for today's leaders."

Quality Digest

"A wonderful collection of practical advice for managers."

Edgar R. Fiedler
Vice President and Economic Counsellor,
The Conference Board

"A great resource tool for business, government, and education."

Dr. Dennis J. Murray
President, Marist College

PRODUCTIVITY PRESS, Dept. BK, PO Box 13390, Portland, OR 97213-0390
Telephone: 1-800-394-6868   Fax: 1-800-394-6286

THE MANAGEMENT MASTER SERIES

The Management Master Series offers business managers leading-edge information on the best contemporary management practices. Written by respected authorities, each short "briefcase book" addresses a specific topic in a concise, to-the-point presentation, using both text and illustrations. These are ideal books for busy managers who want to get the whole message quickly.

Great Management Ideas

Management Alert: Don't Reform—Transform!
Michael J. Kami
Transform your corporation: adapt faster, be more productive, perform better.

Vision, Mission, Total Quality: Leadership Tools for Turbulent Times
William F. Christopher
Build your vision and mission to achieve world class goals.

The Power of Strategic Partnering
Eberhard E. Scheuing
Take advantage of the strengths in your customer-supplier chain.

New Performance Measures
Brian H. Maskell
Measure service, quality, and flexibility with methods that address your customers' needs.

Motivating Superior Performance
Saul W. Gellerman
Use these key factors—non-monetary as well as monetary—to improve employee performance.

Doing and Rewarding: Inside a High-Performance Organization
Carl G. Thor
Design systems to reward superior performance and encourage productivity.

PRODUCTIVITY PRESS, Dept. BK, PO Box 13390, Portland, OR 97213-0390
Telephone: 1-800-394-6868   Fax: 1-800-394-6286

Total Quality

The 16-Point Strategy for Productivity and Total Quality
William F. Christopher/Carl G. Thor
Essential points you need to know to improve the performance of your organization.

The TQM Paradigm: Key Ideas That Make It Work
Derm Barrett
Get a firm grasp of the world-changing ideas beyond the Total Quality movement.

Process Management: A Systems Approach to Total Quality
Eugene H. Melan
Learn how a business process orientation will clarify and streamline your organization's capabilities.

Practical Benchmarking for Mutual Improvement
Carl G. Thor
Discover a down-to-earth approach to benchmarking and building useful partnerships for quality.

Mistake-Proofing: Designing Errors Out
Richard B. Chase and Douglas M. Stewart
Learn how to eliminate errors and defects at the source with inexpensive *poka-yoke* devices and staff creativity.

Communicating, Training, and Developing for
Quality Performance
Saul W. Gellerman
Gain quick expertise in communication and employee development basics.

PRODUCTIVITY PRESS, Dept. BK, PO Box 13390, Portland, OR 97213-0390
Telephone: 1-800-394-6868   Fax: 1-800-394-6286

Customer Focus

Designing Products and Services That Customers Want
Robert King
Here are guidelines for designing customer-exciting products and services to meet the demands for continuous improvement and constant innovation to satisfy customers.

Creating Customers for Life
Eberhard E. Scheuing
Learn how to use quality function deployment to meet the demands for continuous improvement and constant innovation to satisfy customers.

Building Bridges to Customers
Gerald A. Michaelson
From the priceless value of a single customer to balancing priorities, Michaelson delivers a powerful guide for instituting a customer-based culture within any organization.

Delivering Customer Value: It's Everyone's Job
Karl Albrecht
This volume is dedicated to empowering people to deliver customer value and aligning a company's service systems.

Shared Expectations: Sustaining Customer Relationships
Wayne A. Little
How to create a process for sharing expectations and building lasting and profitable relationships with customers and suppliers that incorporates performance goals and measures.

Service Recovery: Fixing Broken Customers
Ron Zemke
Here are the guidelines for developing a customer-retaining service recovery system that can be a strategic asset in a company's total quality effort.

PRODUCTIVITY PRESS, Dept. BK, PO Box 13390, Portland, OR 97213-0390
Telephone: 1-800-394-6868   Fax: 1-800-394-6286

Leadership

Leading the Way to Organization Renewal
Burt Nanus
How to build and steer a continually renewing and transforming organization by applying a vision to action strategy.

Checklist for Leaders
Gabriel Hevesi
Learn to focus day-to-day decisions and actions, leadership, communications, team building, planning, and efficiency.

Creating Leaders for Tomorrow
Karl Albrecht
How to mobilize all the intelligence of the organization to create value for customers.

Total Quality: A Framework for Leadership
D. Otis Wolkins
Consider the problems and opportunities in today's world of changing technology, global competition, and rising customer expectations in terms of the leadership role.

From Management to Leadership
Lawrence M. Miller
A visionary analysis of the qualities required of leaders in today's business: vision and values, enthusiasm for customers, teamwork, and problem-solving skills at all levels.

High Performance Leadership: Creating Value in a World of Change
Leonard R. Sayles
Examine the need for leadership involvement in work systems and operations technology to meet the increasing demands for short development cycles and technologically complex products and services.

PRODUCTIVITY PRESS, Dept. BK, PO Box 13390, Portland, OR 97213-0390
Telephone: 1-800-394-6868   Fax: 1-800-394-6286

ABOUT PRODUCTIVITY PRESS

Productivity Press exists to support the continuous improvement of American business and industry.

Since 1983, Productivity has published more than 100 books on the world's best manufacturing methods and management strategies. Many Productivity Press titles are direct source materials translated for the first time into English from industrial leaders around the world.

The impact of the Productivity publishing program on Western industry has been profound. Leading companies in virtually every industry sector use Productivity Press books for education and training. These books ride the cutting edge of today's business trends and include books on total quality management (TQM), corporate management, Just-In-Time manufacturing process improvements, total employee involvement (TEI), profit management, product design and development, total productive maintenance (TPM), and system dynamics.

To get a copy of the full-color catalog, call 800-394-6868 or fax 800-394-6286.

To view sample chapters and see the complete line of books, visit the Productivity Press online catalog on the Internet at *http://www.ppress.com/*

Productivity Press titles are distributed to the trade by National Book Network, 800-462-6420

TO ORDER: Write, phone, or fax Productivity Press, Dept. BK, P.O. Box 13390, Portland, OR 97213-0390, phone 800-394-6868, fax 800-394-6286. Send check or charge to your credit card (American Express, Visa, MasterCard accepted).

TO ORDER: Write, phone, or fax Productivity Press, Dept. BK, P.O. Box 13390, Portland, OR 97213-0390, phone 1-800-394-6868, fax 1-800-394-6286. Send check or charge to your credit card (American Express, Visa, MasterCard accepted).

U.S. ORDERS: Add $5 shipping for first book, $2 each additional for UPS surface delivery. Add $5 for each AV program containing 1 or 2 tapes; add $12 for each AV program containing 3 or more tapes. We offer attractive quantity discounts for bulk purchases of individual titles; call for more information.

ORDER BY E-MAIL: Order 24 hours a day from anywhere in the world. Use either address:
To order: *service@ppress.com*
To view the online catalog and/or order:
  http://www.ppress.com/

QUANTITY DISCOUNTS: For information on quantity discounts, please contact our sales department.

INTERNATIONAL ORDERS: Write, phone, or fax for quote and indicate shipping method desired. For international callers, telephone number is 503-235-0600 and fax number is 503-235-0909. Prepayment in U.S. dollars must accompany your order (checks must be drawn on U.S. banks). When quote is returned with payment, your order will be shipped promptly by the method requested.

NOTE: Prices are in U.S. dollars and are subject to change without notice.